Local Money

What difference does it make?

John Rogers

Published in this first edition in 2013 by:

Triarchy Press
Station Offices
Axminster
Devon
EX13 5PF
United Kingdom

+44 (0)1297 631456
info@triarchypress.com
www.triarchypress.com

A catalogue record for this book is available from the British
Library.

Print ISBN: 978-1-909470-19-4

Contents

Introduction

In September 2012, Bristol launched its own currency. Brixton, Lewes, Totnes and Stroud have done the same. But what does it mean? What's the point of having 'local' money?

Local money isn't a new idea – it has been in use for most of history. Yet people are not aware of the benefits that local currencies bring to thousands of communities around the world today.

For example, the following polls appeared in the national press after a group of citizens launched the Bristol Pound in September 2012:

The *Daily Telegraph* asked its readers: "If your town launched its own currency, would you use it?"

> 54.2% said Yes
> 45.8% said No

A similar poll in the *Guardian* newspaper asked the question: "Do you think local currencies are a good idea?"

> 38% said Yes
> 62% said No

The conclusion must be that local money is widely misunderstood. Surely we would support a currency that:

- creates new jobs and protects existing ones

- creates and grows businesses

- values and rewards essential work in the community

- reduces our impact on the environment
- protects regions or communities against speculators
- says thank you to young people and other volunteers
- creates resilient, sustainable communities
- provides and gets support for the young and the old.

The purpose of this pamphlet is to explain how local currencies work. Alone they cannot solve all the multiple financial, social and environmental crises we face, but they are an increasingly important part of the answer.

I hope to show you how local money benefits you, your local businesses and your region. I'll name the problems as well as the benefits, and you'll discover the practical difference between national and local currency. Finally, I will give you tips on what actions you can take.

You can use this pamphlet as a personal guide, in a local study group or at a school or college. Sample questions for study groups can be found on pages 61 and 62.

John Rogers

Chapter One

Local Money in Action

Let me tell you a simple story about how local money works. These are the participants:

- **Jennifer** runs a thriving high street and internet business selling traditional homemade food and employs three people. Her goals are to create great products and provide jobs.

- **Jill** works for Jennifer and rents a flat from Graham.

- **Graham** inherited a property from his Mum and rents it out to Jill. He works in a local builder's merchants and has been a lifelong supporter of the Lions football club.

- **The Lions** football club has several volunteer coaches and Jennifer does the catering.

- **Harry** is unemployed but an active member of the community.

- **The Community Bank** exists to create loans in both national currency and Local Pounds. It also hosts a **Community Time Bank** to reward volunteers.

- **The Local Authority** provides a range of public services.

- **Community volunteers**

Jennifer had been running a successful market stall for over a year. She decided to expand her homemade food business by renting a shop in the high street. She secured two loans from her **Community Bank** – £2,000 (at 6% interest) + 2,000 Local Pounds (interest-free). She used the national currency to buy extra equipment; she used the Local Pounds to buy local produce, to pay part of her first wage bills and to pay her rates.

Like most of the shops and businesses in the area, Jennifer accepts payment for her goods in Local Pounds, UK Pounds, or a mix of the two.

Jill works for Jennifer and likes her salary to be part paid in Local Pounds. She pays some of her rent in Local Pounds to her landlord **Graham**. He uses this to pay local builders for any maintenance work, to buy locally, and sometimes he makes donations to **The Lions** amateur football club. The club earns Local Pounds by hiring out its minibus, equipment and meeting rooms, and uses this income to reward its coaches and to pay Jennifer's company for catering services.

Local businesses are able to pay their rates in Local Pounds. **The local authority** uses this income for essential maintenance work on its buildings and to support local community projects. It also provides car parking, local bus services, childcare and after school clubs, all of which can be paid for with Local Pounds and the people who provide the services are partly paid in Local Pounds.

This is a story of a thriving local economy in action, powered by two currencies working hand in hand. The

Local Pounds do not replace UK Pounds but work alongside them. Jennifer put local currency to work by taking an interest-free loan. Other businesses, or individuals, take part by accepting payment for their labour, goods and services in Local Pounds, with a choice of cash (with the same security features as bank notes), electronic card or pay-by-text with a mobile phone.

The same Community Bank that issued the loans to Jennifer also rewards community volunteers with another type of local currency, called Time Credits. This is how they are used in the community...

> *Harry* *is out of work but wants to use his skills to help others in the community. He listed his carpentry skills in the community website directory and has had many requests for help. For each hour of work he receives one time credit. He also helps out with the Wildlife Club, where* ***volunteers*** *receive time credits for litter picks, river clean-ups and species counts.*
>
> *The local Allotments Association has also mobilised many people to form work gangs to create new Community Gardens, all rewarded with time credits.*
>
> *Inmates of the local prison can earn time credits, through work such as refurbishing bicycles, and send the credits out to their families in the community.*
>
> *Time credits can be exchanged at the food bank, supported by a local charity and supermarket. (Any unemployment benefits are not affected because time credits are exempt for both tax and benefits.)*

> *Volunteers who do not want a reward give their credits to other people or put their credits into a community pot to create grants to local groups.*
>
> *Senior citizens can teach young people new skills or help them with their homework and use the credits they earn to get help with their gardening, shopping, household tasks or computer skills etc.*

Although that is just a story of local money in action, everything in it is happening in a local currency system somewhere in the world today. The money is circulating via local people, businesses and voluntary organisations, making its way into the local authority's accounts and out again into the community.

People can start businesses, create jobs, reward volunteers, learn new skills and keep old ones alive, make new friends and connections, and keep active – all essential for healthy individuals, communities and economies.

Maybe you care deeply about the environment or other global issues, or you feel strongly about your local region or community, but you just don't see how local money can help. I hope that this pamphlet will show you connections between what you care about and 'the money problem'.

Visual Resources:
Why the Bristol Pound?
www.youtube.com/watch?v=QtGEby4ORGM
Why Banco Palmas?
www.youtube.com/watch?v=s7t7kdINLP8

Chapter Two

National Money –
what it can and cannot do

Knowing who creates money and why is key to understanding the need for local currencies. First, let's look at the importance of national money.

What can national money do?

National money allows us to meet the complex needs of a modern nation. We can use it to build roads, hospitals and schools, to start and run businesses, to trade with each other, to pay or earn wages, to pay taxes, and to clear debts. This versatility is its greatest strength.

A single national currency gives everyone living in that country a standard currency to carry out their business.

It has three main jobs to do:

1. To provide a recognisable unit of account.
   One UK Pound is the recognised 'legal tender' currency of the United Kingdom. People settle debts and pay taxes to government with reference to this unit of account.

2. To provide a medium of exchange for trade.
   People buy and sell products and services using UK Pounds anywhere in the world, where the currency is accepted. They can also trade it for other internationally recognised currencies.

3. To provide a medium for savings. People earn income now and save any surplus to expand a business, buy a house, invest in a pension or make other future purchases. The interest mechanism means that the money saved can 'grow' or, at the very least, keep pace with inflation.

This kind of description can be found in a standard economics textbook. It describes the 'functions' of money. What it masks is the story of who creates and controls money and for what purpose.

We often think of national money as something that is scarce or abundant – you either have it or you don't; the economy is either booming or in recession. Here's why.

Bank notes and coins are minted by the government and make up just 3% of the 'money supply'.[1] The rest, 97% of modern money, is put into circulation by banks and building societies through *loans*.

Most people believe that banks only lend out money that others have deposited, but this 'common sense' is wrong. The authors of *Where Does Money Come From?* explain:

> The textbook model of banking implies that banks need depositors to start the money creation process. The reality, however, is that when a bank makes a loan it does not require anyone else's money to do so. Banks do not wait for deposits in order to make loans. Bank deposits are created by banks purely on the basis of their own confidence in the capacity

[1] Ryan-Collins, Greenham, Werner & Jackson, *Where Does Money Come From?*, (2nd edition, 2012), pp.6&15 & Positive Money Campaign: www.bit.ly/localmoneyE

> of the borrower to repay the loan... In the
> UK, there are currently no direct compulsory
> cash-reserve requirements placed on banks or
> building societies to restrict their lending.[2]

(At the time of the financial crisis, for example, banks held just £1.25 in reserve for every £100 issued as credit.[3])

If you ask for a loan, the bank will check your 'creditworthiness', based on your current salary, reputation or assets. People who have more assets to begin with have easier access to extra funds because they are seen as 'creditworthy'. They have an advantage over those with no assets. The more assets they have, the more able they are to get more money and use it to earn even more money.

Once a loan is agreed, the bank enters the money as a credit in your account. How? It creates the money at the touch of a computer key – out of thin air (only backed by your legally binding promise to repay). Sounds crazy but it's the truth, confirmed by no less an authority than the Bank of England.[4] Banks have an exclusive licence from the government to 'make' money. It is loans from the banks which bring this new money into circulation, and businesses and individuals are able to use the money to create economic activity.

Banks do not create money for the public good. They are businesses owned by private shareholders. Their purpose is to make a profit. They make a profit by charging *interest* on loans. That interest is used to cover their costs of doing business, all the overheads of administration,

---

2 *ibid* p.20
3 *ibid* p.7
4 *ibid* p.17 & Governor of the Bank of England confirms money creation process: www.bit.ly/localmoneyE

maintaining buildings and employing staff. Plus, they must make a profit for their shareholders.

Businesses and individuals must compete for work to earn enough to pay off their loans. As long as the economy is growing and you have a job or a successful business, you can service your debts. If the economy dives and you can't even pay off the interest, the interest will keep on growing in the form of compound interest.

So, we all pay the price for our need for money to stay alive, buy essentials, travel, do business. And the banks make a profit on our need.

Everyone's in debt

There is 'good' debt (based on kindness) and 'bad' debt (based on interest). The good kind is the favours we all owe each other in families and communities. "I owe you", "I'm in your debt", "How can I ever repay you?". This kind of 'debt' is what really makes the world go round. Without it our communities would fall apart.

The bad kind of debt is created when people with money lend it out or banks create it from nothing, both expecting the money to be returned with interest. People can too easily become debt 'slaves' in such a system. But the whole nation is also a kind of debt slave.

The Bank of England was formed in 1694 by public subscription to lend £1.2 million to rebuild the navy... and the nation began to run up a debt. The national debt has risen sharply after every major war – £850 million by the end of the Napoleonic Wars, £7.4 billion by the end of the First World War and £24.7 billion by the end of the Second World War.[5] In 2013, the national debt stands at

5 National Statistics Office: www.bit.ly/localmoneyF

over £1 trillion. It just keeps on growing. Clearly nobody involved in this scheme ever expects the debt to be paid off. Governments of all types constantly talk about 'reducing the deficit'[6] but in reality all they can hope to do is put the brakes on the speed at which the debt grows.

Behind the national debt stands an army of investors who have lent money to the government expecting their 'return'. Many of these are large institutional investors like pension and insurance funds who need low risk investments (the government has never defaulted on its debts). Interest on the debt in 2013 is £45 billion a year, which is the same amount as we spend on defence. According to the current UK government's own projections:

> Unless borrowing is reduced, interest on Government debt will hit £70 billion a year by 2014-15. This is more than is currently raised from council tax, business rates, stamp duty and inheritance tax combined.[7]

The Bank of England is also banker to local government. Local authorities pay for salaries and other revenue activities through local rates but they fund any building projects or other capital investments from the National Loans Fund. In the financial year 2011/2012 UK local authorities were in debt to a total of £81.8 billion.[8] Scottish citizens paid £700 million in interest on £14 billion of local authority debt in 2012.[9] Check out your local authority's debts here: www.bit.ly/localmoney2

6 Definition of 'deficit reduction': www.bit.ly/localmoneyG
7 www.bit.ly/localmoneyH
8 www.bit.ly/localmoneyI
9 www.bit.ly/localmoneyJ

In the current debt crisis local councils are having to make cuts to many services. The closing of libraries, bus services and many initiatives in the charitable and voluntary sector are all well-known. And, as interest payments on the national debt mount, central government will also have less to spend on providing the services that our regions and local communities need.

To grow or not to grow?

The requirement to pay interest is one of the reasons that economists call for constant growth. If the economy stops growing, businesses fail, people lose their jobs, have less to spend and the economy spirals down into recession.

There are many other forces driving growth too: the need to pay off investments in, say, plant and machinery; rapid population growth; raised expectations of poorer countries to 'catch up' with richer countries; greed. All of these forces lead to increased pressure on the finite environmental resources of our planet.

Economic growth can be either benign or malignant. Growth that relies on natural resources clearly has limits. If you fish all the fish in the sea, you will have no fishing industry. Malignant growth eventually destroys what it feeds off.

Benign growth does not destroy its host but lives in balance with it. Growth is possible in knowledge, intellectual property, human services, renewable energies etc. and can generate shareable wealth.

Gambling or trade?

When banks are cautious, they lend carefully to those who already have assets or guaranteed income. But once money is used for speculation rather than primarily as a medium for trade, the whole system gets skewed in favour of gambling.

The 'credit crunch' was caused by banks creating too much 'easy money' (out of thin air) that was not backed by productive activity. Financial salesmen were very creative at selling 'toxic' debts on to more gullible customers. Everyone hoped someone else would be left standing when the music stopped playing and the chairs were pulled away.[10]

Ten years before the current crisis, voices already warned of the dangers of gigantic credit bubbles, but they were ignored as party-poopers. Mainstream politics, media and economics were dominated by group-think and denial. A year into the crisis, the International Monetary Fund (IMF) – the world's financial police force – published a paper showing that there were 124 systemic banking crises, 208 currency crises and 63 episodes of sovereign debt defaults between 1970 and 2007.[11]

So we can hardly say that financial crises are new. It was only the scale of the events of 2008 that was unexpected.

What can national money not do?

National money can't promise us a *stable* unit of exchange. How much, say, £5 is worth for purchasing real goods and services depends on speculation through the money markets.

> Today's foreign exchange and financial
> derivatives markets dwarf anything else on
> our planet. In 2010, the volume of foreign

10 For a great visualisation of the 'sub-prime mortgage' scam and the ensuing credit bubble in the USA: www.bit.ly/localmoneyK

11 IMF Working Paper, L.Laeven & F.Valencia 'Systemic Banking Crises: A New Database', (2008), www.bit.ly/localmoneyL

exchange transactions reached $4 trillion *per day*. One day's exports or imports of *all* goods and services in the world amount to about 2% of that figure. Which means that 98% of transactions on these markets are purely speculative. This foreign exchange figure does not include derivatives, whose notional volume was $600 trillion – or eight times the entire world's *annual* GDP in 2010.[12]

Many of the 208 currency crises noted by the IMF since 1970 were sparked by currency speculators.

National money can't protect us from abuses of power. Money is intimately linked to power. Wealthy people can buy influence with political parties and pervert democratic processes. As citizens, we all in theory control 'our' national currency: we elect governments which appoint the officials of the Bank of England who manage the nation's money supply. In practice you and I have no control over their decisions. If the Bank of England decides to create money to go to war or to bail out other banks, we cannot affect these decisions.

National money tends to be scarce. Even when the economy is booming, national currency is designed to be relatively scarce in order to maintain its value. Since the financial crisis that began in 2008, money has been more scarce than usual, banks have been very cautious about lending, economic activity has decreased and the UK government has been cutting funding for public services. Bank profits are not being circulated in the economy but in the global casino of speculation.

---

12 Lietaer et al, *Money and Sustainability – the Missing Link*, (2012), p11-12

It is the government, the banks and their shareholders which control whether there is enough money for you or your community to do whatever is necessary to meet its needs – so, it could be a long wait until any funding arrives.

National money subject to interest cannot prevent inequalities. The system of wealth 'creation' through bank loans based on 'creditworthiness' and compound interest perpetuates a system where the rich tend to get richer and the poor get poorer; inequality and all the social problems that go with it tend to rise. Government spending then has to address this inequality by providing education, healthcare and welfare services. You can see how UK tax is allocated at www.wheredoesmymoneygo. org/dailybread.html

National money cannot ensure a level playing field between the regions. National money serves the needs of the nation but regions must compete for a share of the national currency pie.

Remember – 97% of money is working to create a profit for the banks and investors. So the present monetary system acts like a pump, siphoning capital from the regions in which it is earned and transferring it to where it will earn the greatest profit, anywhere on the planet. If that is not in your region, it will never arrive.

Currency at this scale is vast and anonymous and is not designed to meet the needs of regions and communities.

Chapter Three

Can we reform money?

Everyone is waiting for money. National currency is scarce because its creators keep it scarce. So people are experimenting with new ideas for issuing and organising money.

The Positive Money Campaign[1] uses video and blogging to present the problems of a private banking monopoly. These monetary reformers say that government could issue interest-free, debt-free money itself – through a specially appointed central committee – without borrowing from private banks at interest and running an unpayable national debt. They argue that we should take away the power of creating credit 'out of thin air' from private banks and give it to government.[2]

Centralised debt-free money issuance may be a partial solution to running national services like education and health but it can never be a solution for lack of money at the local level. Local communities would still be dependent on a government committee for how much money was allocated to their region.

---

1 Positive Money Reforms in Plain English: www.bit.ly/localmoneyM
2 *Gizmag* article "300 million dollars out of thin air: Bitcoin turns four and approaches $30 value"; www.bit.ly/localmoneyN

Virtual currencies?

'Virtual currencies' are not new – various attempts have been made since the mid-1990s to create a viable system. These types of currency only operate online, have no physical tokens and are issued by a private organisation or collective rather than a government or bank. Amazon, Facebook and many others are currently experimenting with them. Recently, a currency called Bitcoin has been making waves. Started in 2009, it is the first virtual currency to get such widespread attention.

New Bitcoins are created by computers solving difficult equations through complicated algorithms; each newly 'mined' unit of currency is checked for validity by the global network and then spent into circulation so ownership can be verified. There is a set limit on how many new 'coins' can be created so the total possible money supply is strictly controlled.

Supporters of Bitcoin claim it is a radical 'game changer', a big improvement on inflation-ridden national currencies, creating a stable currency because the money supply can't be arbitrarily increased by printing new money.

Critics have three main arguments against it: trust in an 'un-hackable' algorithm is as naïve as trust in a central bank because sooner or later someone with superior technical skills will work out how to crack it; early adopters who created lots of currency on their computers already seem to be manipulating a speculative bubble with bitcoins selling at high prices in national currencies – some estimate that more than 75 percent of all bitcoins are being hoarded instead of being spent[15]; deflation is built into the currency because the designers put a deliberate cap on how much could ever be created – so as more and more businesses and consumers adopt it as a medium of exchange there will be too many goods and services pursuing too little currency.[3]

Local Money

So, what are the arguments for and against local money? Here is a summary, based on the comments which followed the polls (in the introduction) on both the Telegraph and Guardian websites[4] after the launch of both the Bristol Pound in 2012 and the Brixton Pound in September 2009.

Supporters say that local currencies:

- create local wealth and keep it local (rather than it going to distant shareholders and corporations that have no interest in the area other than to make money)
- circulate around the local area more times than national currency and so can do more economic good – the 'multiplier effect'
- help small independent retailers
- value and reward people who contribute to the community's common good

---

3 For a full discussion of arguments for and against Bitcoin, see the P2P Foundation site: www.bit.ly/localmoneyV

4 *Daily Telegraph*, "Bristol launches local currency": www.bit.ly/localmoneyA

Guardian, "Bristol banks on alternative pound": www.bit.ly/localmoneyB

Guardian, "Are Local Currencies a good idea?": www.bit.ly/localmoneyC

Guardian, "Will the Brixton Pound work?": www.bit.ly/localmoneyD

- make skills and tools more widely available
- encourage businesses that are rooted in the community, source local products and employ local people
- give regions an economic tool to weather recessions through increased money supply and protection of jobs and businesses
- provide a more stable and fairer means of money creation than a private banking and financial system based on speculation.

Opponents of local currencies think that:

- they are just a gimmick or middle-class fad
- they are useless to local businesses with supply chains outside the area
- local shops should concentrate on giving better service if they want to survive
- if you want money to be spent in your area, you should produce something
- they are useless to people on low incomes who shop at low price supermarkets that do not take part in the local currency
- people can just use national currency to support local businesses so the extra trouble of a local currency is unnecessary
- they are an attack on free trade and the free movement of goods and services without boundaries
- local currencies could create unfair competition, local monopolies and corruption

- you cannot pay national taxes or settle legal debts with them so they are of limited appeal
- we could not have developed the Apple computer or sent a man to the moon with local currencies.

(I give answers to these objections in Chapter Five.)

Some of the arguments put forward to support local currencies may seem 'idealistic'. But they are based on fact – there are already hundreds of local currencies doing some or all of those things somewhere in the world.

Local currency is one of those great ideas that has the potential to change how we think and act. The existing reality always seems 'normal', the way we have always done things, reliable, safe. But think about other ideas that seemed idealistic or innovative at the time.

A hundred years ago the idea of workers, women or ethnic minorities having the right to vote or other civil rights seemed wildly utopian. Now these are the basic rights of all citizens in democracies.

Credit cards were also a disruptive innovation in the 1960s. Until then, cash and cheques were king. Then VISA revolutionised credit through its unique international clearing system operated through participating banks. Now millions of people use credit cards to carry out their daily business.

Chapter Four

Local Money– what it can and cannot do

Who creates local money and why?

We can always create enough of our own local money to handle all the trades and exchanges we wish to make. While national currency basically drives, and is driven by, profit, local money supports people with other values: people who believe in local diversity, mutual help, treating people as assets instead of problems, valuing all types of work, creating strong social networks and protecting the environment. It is these people, their values and commitment that make local money systems work.

Local currencies work in parallel with national currencies. They are interest-free and give us easy access to a medium of exchange for local trade *that is not depleted by interest repayments. It maintains its value and circulates quickly, creating more economic activity*.

A wide range of groups have set up various kinds of local currencies for a variety of reasons:

- business to business trade networks have been created to share spare business capacity
- citizens and neighbours set up Local Exchange Trading Systems (LETS) or Time Banks to support community and neighbourliness or to help the vulnerable

- residents of a Brazilian slum started Banco Palmas to get access to microcredit in both national and local currency
- voluntary organisations create local currencies to help a range of clients: young people; elderly people; people with disabilities and mental health problems; residents of housing associations
- local governments support local currencies to enable their local area to thrive; they have accepted them for payment of local business rates in Brixton, Bristol, Nantes in France and Vorarlberg in Austria, for example.

Business exchange networks are usually run as for-profit enterprises, which charge participants various fees. All other types of local currency are run as not-for-profit enterprises.[1]

Healthy geographical boundaries for local money

A local economy can remain healthy if it has healthy boundaries to its flow of money. If too much escapes from the region into the pockets of distant corporations and governments, the local economy is weakened.

A local money system draws a big fat line around a region and says: "only valid here". You cannot easily spend your Bristol Pound in London or your Brixton Pound in Glasgow unless someone there is willing to accept it for trade.

So, what are the main advantages of a geographical boundary?

- The money stays to do more work in your region

---

1 Kennedy, M., Lietaer, B., Rogers, J., *People Money – the Promise of Regional Currencies*. (2012) contains details about all the main types of system in operation today.

– the 'multiplier effect' – instead of disappearing into banks and the money 'casino'.

- Local money encourages local diversity, quality and identity.
- Local money supports local start-up businesses, jobs and production.

Local businesses with suppliers from outside their region use their national currency for these suppliers and earn local money to pay local suppliers.

Healthy ethical boundaries for local money

Another boundary is an ethical one. Our high streets are dominated by the same chain stores owned by corporations with anonymous, distant shareholders.[2]

Some systems are totally open about their response to this. The world's largest local money system, the Swiss WIR Bank, does not allow discounters or department stores that are seen as damaging to their sector to take part. Others implicitly exclude large chains by focussing their marketing efforts on small local enterprises with local supply chains, organic and fair trade businesses and social enterprises. Some systems exclude particular types of trades in their terms of business or trading rules and expel members found to be in breach of them.

What can local currency do?

Local currencies provide the means for increased economic activity to take place alongside the national currency, particularly when the latter is scarce.

For example, a restaurant may regularly have empty seats because high unemployment and the financial

2 Clone Town Britain, New Economics Foundation: www.bit.ly/localmoneyP

29

squeeze mean that many people haven't got the money to eat there. Instead of lowering its prices, it can offer meals in whole or part for local currency. (Remember that local currency can be earned by unemployed people working in the community and others who are unable to find (enough) regular work that is paid in national currency.) This is additional income with which the restaurant can buy food from local food producers, or pay part of its staff wages or pay its business rates. This same principle can be applied to hotels, meeting rooms, cinema, theatre and concert tickets, equipment, vehicles, etc. Wherever businesses are operating below capacity, or where there are underused assets belonging to voluntary organisations or local government, these can be tapped to bring in extra trade or other benefits to the organisation.

People and businesses earn local currency through offering their services and exchange it for other services that they wouldn't otherwise have been able to afford. They can buy food, pay rent, pay for transport, pay for energy services and get help of all kinds. Personal skills and talents are valued and businesses have another platform for trade.

The flexibility in the design of local currencies means that they can be used to meet very particular needs in the region. For instance, a group of people may want to create a community garden for both health and environmental benefits. They may not have enough national currency to pay people but they can mobilise people to help with the work by offering rewards through a local currency. There are many other systems in operation that benefit different groups in the community or meet special needs: schools; community education; users of a doctor's surgery; environmental projects; disaster relief; intentional communities.[3]

Local currencies are designed to make sure that currency keeps circulating and keeps working. This is why organisers discourage positive interest payments and some even build in 'negative interest' or a 'hoarding fee' to make the currency lose its value if you hold on to it for too long.

Of course, all of the above benefits are only possible in well-designed systems that are professionally run and managed.

What can local currency not do?

Just like national currency, local currency has limitations. It cannot:

- pay legal debts
- pay national taxes
- earn interest (we've just seen why this is)
- be traded on international currency markets.

A short history of local currencies

National currencies are really the new kid on the block. Until the nineteenth century, local currencies and mutual favours were the norm. Gold was used for national and international trade, followed by bank notes and bank accounts. But most people carried out their business as favours – I help you now so you help me later – or used a local currency: wood, copper, brass and silver were all used for local tokens.[4]

---

3 *ibid* p.189-194
4 *ibid* Chapter 3

After the Industrial Revolution, central banking increased the efficiency of national and international trade and national currencies were established as the only 'legal tender' for payment of taxes and debts. This did not make all local currency 'illegal'; it simply stopped private local banks and employers issuing their own notes and tokens and forcing people to use them, which had become common practice.

Citizens, businesses and local government in different parts of the world all issued local currencies during recession periods in the 1930s, 1990s and have done so again in the early 21st century. Experiments in many countries around the world[5] are working successfully in both urban and rural areas and both for people who are cash-rich and time-poor as well as for people on low incomes with time to spare.

The Bank of England recognises that modern local currencies exist. It offers the following guidance on its website:

> 'Local' or 'complementary' currency schemes
> generally aim to promote local economic
> activity by implementing a payment mechanism
> (often including physical vouchers) that can
> be used for purchases from local businesses.
> The concept is that the payment arrangement
> encourages consumers to purchase goods
> and services from local businesses that in
> turn purchase goods and services from local
> suppliers, or pay their staff partly with the local
> currency. The intention is that the scheme
> creates a 'positive multiplier' effect, keeping
> spending within the local area.

---

5 *ibid* p.75-78

Its guidance[6] on local currencies answers several Frequently Asked Questions:

Are local currencies linked to the Bank of England?

Are local currencies legal tender?

I have seen 'notes' issued by local currency schemes – what is the status of these?

In the event that a local currency scheme fails, can I receive compensation from the Bank of England?

How are local currencies issued?

The technicalities of how bank money and Bitcoin are issued are obscure and inaccessible to most people. So how does local currency differ?

First, the body issuing the local currency can either be a privately owned business (like business barter networks) or a collectively owned body with a democratic governance structure (a cooperative, community interest company, charity, etc.). It could also be a local partnership of citizens, businesses, voluntary organisations and local government.

The body which issues the currency can do it in two main ways:

1. The managing body guarantees or backs the currency in some way:

   ° with national currency – you buy local currency with national currency and spend it into circulation; you can sell it back for national currency (e.g.Brixton and Bristol Pounds)

---

6 www.bit.ly/localmoneyQ

- ° with the promise of future goods and services (e.g.Equal Dollars, USA)
- ° with rewards like trips, time at the theatre, etc. (e.g.Blaengarw Time Centre)
- ° with future electricity consumption, (see 'Energising Money', www.bit.ly/localmoney3)
- ° with precious metals like gold or silver (e.g. Liberty Dollar)

Currency is issued as circulating notes or vouchers and/or as electronic currency for use online or through mobile devices.

2. The managing body provides a 'mutual credit' accounting system to record all transactions with transparent accounts. Traders issue credit when they trade. All negative and positive account balances equal to zero. Traders promise to return services to the whole trading community, not to any single individual they trade with. Examples of this kind of system are WIR Bank and Business Barter Networks (www.irta.com), Local Exchange Trading Systems (www.letslinkuk.net) and Time Banks (www.timebanking.org).

Local Currencies in Action

Let's see what modern local currencies can really do by looking at some examples from around the world. In Chapter One we saw eight benefits of highly effective local currencies to:

- create new businesses
- create new jobs
- get loans for production and consumption

- reward volunteers for service to the community
- help protect the local environment
- engage young people
- help elderly people
- pay local taxes.

The following profiles of local currencies are from England, Wales, Switzerland, Brazil and the USA. Each of these systems has been designed to meet a purpose within a local or regional area and achieves some of the above benefits; some come close to achieving all of them.

The WIR Bank is 79 years old; Equal Dollars is 18 years old; Banco Palmas is 15 years old; Blaengarw Time Centre is 7 years old; Brixton Pound is 3.5 years old. Each system has shown different degrees of staying power. (You can read more about these systems and many others, based on interviews with local organisers, in our book *People Money – the Promise of Regional Currencies*, which also contains more details about different models, mechanisms and design processes.)

Brixton Pound, London

Local Markets in the Inner City
www.brixtonpound.org

This is the youngest of our examples. The Brixton Pound was started in September 2009 and serves a multi-cultural inner city area in the London borough of Lambeth. The B£ aims to:

- protect the jobs and livelihoods of Brixton residents through developing a diverse and resilient local economy in the face of a recession and chain store dominance
- raise community awareness of the local Brixton economy and encourage a self-help attitude
- encourage local sourcing of goods to decrease CO_2 emissions
- raise Brixton's profile regionally and nationally and contribute to positive perceptions of Brixton by drawing attention to its strong community, diverse economy and capacity for innovation.

(A video link to how it works can be found here: www.bit.ly/Brixton£)

How is it doing in 2013? [7]

A total of B£75,000 in notes and B£e60,000 in electronic currency has been issued since 2009.

Protecting jobs and livelihoods: In early 2013, there were over 1,000 participants: 840 registered individuals, 108 businesses and 8 charities for the Pay-by-Text service; 250 businesses accept circulating notes. A wide variety of

[7] Figures from an interview with Sue Steed, a former volunteer and board member with the Brixton Pound, who works with local currencies at the New Economics Foundation in London.

businesses have joined: restaurants, cafes, pubs, market traders, book and stationery shops, grocers shops, flower stalls, hardware and garden stores, solicitors, sports shops, therapists and dry cleaners.[8]

Market traders and mobile businesses like hairdressers and therapists say they find the electronic Pay-by-Text service is easier to use and more reliable than credit cards.

Electronic Brixton Pounds are much easier to track than the circulating notes and over two thirds of these units have been re-spent at least once by a business. In total there has been £100,000 value of transactions in B£e giving a velocity of around 1.7 (the value of transactions divided by the amount of money in the system).

Some initial research done by the New Economics Foundation with a sample of businesses that used the notes found they had a local economic multiplier of 1.76. This means that for every B£1 spent in those businesses an additional B£0.76 goes into the local economy.[9]

In a recent survey of participating businesses:

- 69% of respondents were very satisfied or quite satisfied with the scheme

- 35% felt it has increased footfall (with 30% not being sure).

- 80% of respondents said they would recommend the scheme to other Brixton businesses.

Raising community awareness of the local Brixton economy: Organisers provide the network so that residents, businesses, voluntary organisations and the

---

8 For a full directory of current traders in Brixton Pound:
www.brixtonpound.org/spend/
9 More information on the local multiplier or LM3 here:
www.bit.ly/localmoneyS

local authority can connect with and support each other. In 2012, they conducted a survey of Lambeth Council employees before launching 'Payroll Local' (a scheme where staff can take part of their salary in B£). They wanted to find out what their staff thought about the Brixton Pound.

Some initial results from the survey:

- over 80% of staff surveyed said they thought the B£ was a good way to support independent businesses

- 20% of respondents said they had used the Brixton Pound before

- 234 members of staff were asked if they wanted to take part in Payroll Local, of these 134 said they would like to take some salary as B£

- the average amount pledged per member of staff was £22.24 with a monthly total of £5,205.

This is a good start for raising awareness amongst local authority employees, many of whom live in the borough and have local families. (I hope that an understanding of the money system outlined in this pamphlet will inspire more people to participate.)

Encouraging local sourcing of goods to decrease CO_2 emissions: When goods can be sourced locally, it automatically reduces pollution from transport. A few new local businesses produce locally – a food producer growing food in polytunnels – and, in the spirit of reducing emissions, a service delivering groceries by bicycle are early examples.

The Brixton Pound has also run two series of workshops with people thinking of starting food businesses to try and connect them up with existing businesses that are looking for new supply chains.

Raising Brixton's profile: Brixton Pound's notes feature famous personalities with a connection to Brixton: Vincent van Gogh, David Bowie, James Lovelock and others. Its designs won top prize at the UK's prestigious Marketing Design Awards in 2012. One of the judges said: "It was brilliant to see design being brought to bear in a concept that is seeking to bring about social change and community cohesion".[10] International media coverage of the launch of the Brixton Pound was estimated to be worth £100,000 in free advertising to the borough.

How is Brixton Pound run?

Brixton Pound is governed by a Community Interest Company with an elected board. It employs three part-time staff, accountable to the board. Brixton Pound takes two forms:

* circulating printed notes, 1B£ = £1 Sterling
* pay-by-text electronic currency
  11 B£es = £10 Sterling (this gives participants 10% extra spending power).

People get B£ either by buying them with sterling or by offering their goods and services for payment in B£.

B£ notes have the latest security features and serial numbers; all businesses have a printed users' guide; a 'Users Group' of the B£e discusses any problems and gives feedback to management.

The Brixton Pound is working with Lambeth Council on a project to look at designing a currency that can be used across the whole of Lambeth, as part of an EU project called Community Currencies in Action.[11]

---

10 Brixton Pound wins Marketing Design Awards 2012:
www.bit.ly/localmoneyT
11 www.communitycurrenciesinaction.eu

Blaengarw Time Centre, Wales

Saying THANK YOU to Volunteers
www.bit.ly/blaengarw

The Blaengarw Time Centre launched in 2006. It is based in a refurbished Miners' Welfare Hall and serves an ex-mining village at the top of the Garw valley in the borough of Bridgend in South Wales. It attracts visitors from all over the world.

The Time Centre aims to:

- encourage community participation, ownership and responsibility and bring people together in a spirit of equality

- value and record contributions to community life and get things done that wouldn't otherwise get done

- build people's confidence and skills

- build organisational capacity.

How is it doing in 2013?[12]

Encouraging community participation: The Time Centre has a thousand active community members generating 60,000 hours of service per year. There are 600 visitors to the community hall each week.

Valuing and recording contributions to community life: The Time Centre inspired the first community festival since the closure of the mine in the 1980s. Local volunteers put in 7,000 hours of time in organising the festival, which is now an annual event and a great symbol of the community's revival.

---

12 Figures from an interview with Blaengarw Time Centre co-founder Geoff Thomas.

Building people's confidence and skills: People take part in a wide range of learning opportunities and activities: the community festival; assisting with after school clubs; helping with social events; maintenance; administration; mentoring; delivering leaflets; Street Ambassadors project with local police; summer play schemes; environmental and arts projects; apprenticeships in the Community Café (the Food Studio).

Building organisational capacity: The Time Centre has inspired 15 new or revived social enterprises including a revived Social Club and the Community Café.

How is the Blaengarw Time Centre run?

The Time Centre is run by the Creation Development Trust, a social enterprise that took over the running of the old miners' welfare hall ten years ago. The development trust has professional managers accountable to an annually elected board.

The currency mechanism: one hour of service to the community = one time credit.

Time credits are issued as circulating notes to volunteers in community projects. Notes can be exchanged for services from others or redeemed directly for an hour at a community music or theatre event, an hour at an arts class or at the community café, for example.

WIR Bank, Switzerland

Dual Currency Bank for Small Businesses
www.wir.ch

WIR Bank runs the world's oldest and most successful regional currency. It was founded as an exchange ring for small businesses in 1934 and has an unbroken 79 year trading history. Since the 1990s, it has combined conventional banking activities with its business exchange ring.

The WIR Bank aims to:

- serve the financial needs of businesses and individuals with normal banking services – current accounts; savings accounts; insurance services – in Swiss national currency
- provide an additional medium of exchange – the WIR franc – exclusively to small and medium enterprises (SMEs)
- promote the WIR franc as a marketing instrument and cashless payment medium.

How is it doing in 2013? [13]

Serving the financial needs of businesses and individuals: WIR Bank's Annual Report for 2012 reported a 3.3% increase in business in national currency with record assets of over 4 billion Swiss francs (£2.8 billion). Much of this is due to a boom in the building industry.

Providing an additional medium of exchange – the WIR franc – to SMEs: 60,000 small and medium enterprises (businesses with less than 250 employees)

---

13 WIR Bank 2012 Annual Report: www.bit.ly/localmoneyU

across Switzerland use the second currency, the WIR franc. It is simply an accounting mechanism for participating businesses known as a 'mutual credit' clearing system for debits and credits. There is no circulating currency. One WIR franc is worth one Swiss franc in value. When the main economy is strong and interest rates are low, fewer businesses use the second currency; when the economy is weak and interest rates are high, more businesses use the WIR franc accounting system.

In 2012, the turnover of WIR francs reduced by 6% on the previous year down to 1.5 billion (£1 billion). This is attributed to the currently strong Swiss economy and full order books for many companies in national currency as well as historically low interest rates, which make the interest-free second currency less attractive at the moment.

Promoting the WIR franc as a marketing instrument: SMEs have access to a country-wide business network organised in local chapters. They have access to thousands of categories of goods and services provided by 60,000 SMEs without using national currency. They can pay for a variety of services in WIR francs: business expenses; employees' wages; capital expenditure, e.g. building and renovation work. In some sectors, particularly in the construction industry, workers who accept WIR francs have a competitive advantage in the job market.

How is the WIR Bank run?

WIR Bank has always been run as a co-operative since 1934. Its founding constitution binds it to serve primarily the interests of small and medium enterprises. Larger companies may use WIR Bank's services, including the WIR franc accounting system, but have no voting rights in the co-operative that runs the bank.

This form of governance allows SMEs to maintain control over the organisation. The co-operative employs 205 staff with a headquarters in Basel and seven regional centres.

Banco Palmas, Brazil

Self-organised Dual Currency Banking for the Poor
www.bancopalmas.org.br

Banco Palmas started as a conventional micro-credit
lending service in the Conjunto Palmeiras, a poor area
near the city of Fortaleza in Brazil in 1998. It added its
own currency, the 'Palmas', in 2003. The Banco Palmas
aims to overcome urban poverty through:

- implementing projects and programmes of work
to generate income
- offering loans for production and consumption in
both national and local currency.

How is it doing in 2013? [14]

**Implementing projects and programmes of work to
generate income:** Banco Palmas has supported many
new businesses and hundreds of local jobs.

Palma Tur promotes urban community tourism
to strengthen local economic development and
guarantee work and income for local women

Palma Fashion gives fashion related work
opportunities to women suffering from drug
addiction, domestic violence, and other
difficulties. Palma Fashion produces a diverse
collection of clothing, handbags, shoes and
more.

Palma Limpe produces cleaning materials:
detergent, disinfectant, bleach, fabric softener
and liquid wax, and is run by local young people.

14 This profile is based on an interview with Carlos de Freitas of Palmas
Institute Europe.

45

Palma Natus was created in 2005 and works with handmade soaps and herbal products.

Loja Solidária 'Solidarity Shop' is based in Banco Palmas headquarters and exhibits and sells products manufactured in the neighbourhood. These products are also sold at the weekly Banco Palmas Market, where all products made in the neighbourhood are sold. The 'Palmas' currency is accepted at both venues.

When the Banco Palmas started in 1997, only 20% of residents' purchases were made within the area. By 2011, this was turned around: 93% of local residents' purchases were made in the area, reducing transport costs, food miles and CO_2 footprints and creating work and opportunities for residents.

Offering loans for production and consumption: Thousands of local people have benefited from micro-credit loans in both national and local currency over the last 15 years. Loans are offered in four categories.

1. **Credit for Production, Consumption, or Service:** National currency loans for improving or creating small businesses.

2. **Credit for Productive Inclusion:** Instant credit (national currency) allowing the creditor to benefit from the day-to-day opportunities the community market has to offer.

3. **"Casa Produtiva":** Instant credit (national currency) for the purpose of home renovation, with the objective of creating or improving an income generating enterprise.

4. **Credit for Local Consumption:** Loans in local 'Palmas' currency. The Palmas is backed by the national currency and the exchange between the two currencies is legally permitted. 46,000 Palmas (€20,000) were in circulation in 2011. Local currency circulates through local businesses up to 5 times more than national currency.

How is the Banco Palmas run?

The bank is governed by the Palmas Institute, a non-profit organisation, which employs six full-time staff. There are weekly meetings at which all users of the bank's services can share ideas, opinions, complaints and problems. One Palmas = One Brazilian Real.

It has the support of the Brazilian Central Bank, which has also assisted in the replication of the model. By May 2013, there were 103 Community Banks operating on the Banco Palmas model around the country.

Equal Dollars, USA

Voluntary sector currency
www.equaldollars.org

Equal Dollars is a project of Resources for Human Development (RHD), a multi-million dollar health services 'Common Good Corporation' started in Philadelphia, USA in 1970. The currency was introduced in 1995 and is fully integrated into the corporation. The Equal Dollars currency aims to:

- empower and enrich communities by giving value to unused assets that are undervalued or no longer have value in the national US Dollar economy.

How is it doing in 2013?[15]

Empowering and enriching communities by giving value to unused assets: Equal Dollars runs various programmes to achieve this aim.

> **Business to Business Exchange:** Businesses trade spare capacity in the business sector.

> **Keepin' It Local:** Local residents give service to the community, like litter picks, and get access to good deals on local goods and services in local shops and businesses.

> **Food Market:** Participants earn Equal Dollars by giving service in the community. RHD negotiates deliveries of unsold or unused food from a large food corporation, which it then sells for Equal Dollars to its participants.

---

15 This profile is based on an interview with Bob Fishman and Deneene Brockington of Resources for Human Development.

This gives people on low incomes access to quality food at low prices, stops food waste and empowers people to become valued members of the community.

How is Equal Dollars run?

RHD has integrated Equal Dollars fully into its existing governance structures. It is managed by one full-time manager plus 3 staff. One Equal Dollar = $US 0.80.

Chapter Five

Talking to the Naysayers

What about all those objections to local currencies on the Telegraph and Guardian websites, outlined in Chapter Three? Here are some answers.

They are just a gimmick or middle-class fad. Time Banks, Banco Palmas and Equal Dollars are not middle class. But, some currencies can certainly seem so. New local currencies like the Brixton and Bristol pound will survive if they are useful to a wide range of people with different needs.

They are useless to local businesses with supply chains outside the area. Businesses can use their national currency to pay suppliers outside the area and local currency to pay local suppliers. If all their suppliers are non-local, then the local currency will not help in this particular process. However, small businesses wishing to support the principles of local currency could offer to part pay wages in local currency.

Local shops should concentrate on giving better service if they want to survive. Many local shops give great personal service and still have the odds stacked against them by the tactics of 'big retail' with their 'loss leaders' (like selling bread at much lower prices to lure customers in) and massive marketing budgets.

If you want money to be spent in your area, you should produce something. The extreme mobility of global capital has left many areas full of unemployed people who were once proud producers. They must either move elsewhere to find work or find new ways to produce something locally. Some communities have successfully taken over community assets such as shops, cafes, post offices or community centres and run them as social enterprises for the benefit of the community, creating jobs in the process. Some of these, like the Creation Development Trust and its Blaengarw Time Centre, show how people in ex-industrial areas can regain pride in producing local goods and services, even if it will never be on the scale of the old industries. Ownership of the means of exchange – the local currency – gives them ownership of the means of local production.

They are useless to people on low incomes who shop at low price supermarkets that do not take part in the local currency. Low price supermarkets are unlikely to use local currencies, either because it is not in their interest to do so or because the currency organisers do not want them. But we have seen that the Equal Dollars scheme and Banco Palmas specifically cater for people with low or no incomes and local currency organisers need to make sure that the design of their currency does not exclude people on low incomes.

People can just use national currency to support local businesses so why bother with the extra trouble of a local currency? It's true that many people do indeed support local businesses with national currency, which may circulate in the local economy for a little longer before disappearing into the global marketplace again.

Adding a local currency simply ensures that currency circulates longer in the local economy and brings more benefits to the region. It needs to be easy to understand and easy to use.

They are an attack on free trade and the free movement of goods and services. Local currencies are not designed to replace national currencies, which will continue to encourage and facilitate national and international trade. But globalisation has weakened and damaged many local communities – local currencies can help to redress the balance.

Local currencies could create unfair competition, local monopolies and corruption. The risk of fraud and corruption is far higher in a system based on a for-profit national currency than with one based on a not-for-profit local currency. Well designed and managed local currencies build in many safeguards to ensure a fair local marketplace with sound rules for issuing and retiring currency.

You cannot pay national taxes or settle legal debts with them so they are of limited appeal. People will continue to use national money to pay national taxes and settle their debts. Local currencies are used for other purposes, such as to provide interest-free money to support the community, and for paying local taxes and business rates. Local money is subject to income tax and this can be paid by converting a percentage of local earnings to national currency.

They could not have developed the Apple computer or sent a man to the moon. A local business could produce a prototype of an Apple computer with the help of a local currency, but it's true that products with global demand need extended supply chains facilitated by national currency. Local currencies do not aim to compete in this space.

Chapter Six

What can I do?

I've told you about the benefits and potential of local currencies. When they are well organised, they work extremely well.

So why isn't there a local currency in every town and region of the UK? In reality it takes a lot of work to create a viable local currency: you need to design it well, have a great management team, recover the costs of running the currency itself and convince a critical mass of people to use it.

Local money systems are in a process of evolution. The 79-year-old Swiss WIR Bank has inspired local government in the city of Nantes to create a new currency using the same basic accounting system but widening participation to individuals and the city government itself. The first Transition Town currency in Totnes was a limited experiment that set off a domino effect of similar initiatives in Lewes, Brixton, Stroud and now in Bristol. Each group learns from the mistakes and limitations of others.

There is no one-size-fits-all model of local currency. This allows for diversity and adaptation to unique local needs and circumstances in each region and community.

So what can you do?

There are various ways you can support a local currency. The best way is to use it. Offer your services and spend the currency locally so that you become an active 'prosumer' – both producer and consumer. See how well it works for you.

Go to meetings and learn more about the currency from organisers. If you think the currency could reach more people in the community, make sure your voice is heard and offer to help. Use the information in this pamphlet and our book *People Money* to consider potential improvements.

Ask questions to find out:

- how well the currency is meeting the whole community's needs – the needs of businesses, voluntary groups, and people on low incomes? Are there plans to do more?
- if there any more underused resources in the community? And are there plans to bring them on board?
- how well the community understands the principles and benefits of local currencies?
- how are decisions made? Is governance inclusive?
- whether members know that they can donate local currency to local voluntary organisations engaged in community work?
- whether it is possible to adapt an existing system to maximise its impact, e.g. offering time credits 'under the same roof'?

Most importantly, celebrate the successes of your local currency. Advertise them far and wide. Use people who have benefited from the currency as ambassadors to convince other businesses, individuals and voluntary groups to take part.

Learn the lingo

Twenty years ago I started a local currency with some friends. I was blissfully ignorant of economics and short of money. "Let's make our own", we said! So we did, and it lasted for over fifteen years. It was a great learning experience and I firmly believe that if I *had* been trained in economics or finance, I would never have started. Since then I have learned a lot about money and economics, much of it not in the standard textbooks.

Economics mostly ignores local currencies or dismisses them as irrelevant or counterproductive in a globalised world. Only sociologists and geographers have taken an interest in them.[1] Practice is often ahead of theory in many fields. The Wright brothers got a plane to fly through careful experimentation, the appliance of the known science and dogged persistence.

Local currencies are blazing trails towards new economic and social territory. They are driven by active citizens, businesses and local government who want to make local money systems that help people when national money breaks down or is scarce.

Children learn their native tongue naturally by listening, absorbing, experimenting and getting feedback, not by reading grammar books. Similarly, we 'learn the lingo' of exchange by doing exchanges not by reading economic theories. So get involved and start trading in your local system. If there isn't one, start one.

---

1 You can follow academic research into local currencies at the free International Journal of Community Currency Research:www.ijccr.net

At the same time, it is worth 'learning the lingo' of 'economic growth' to understand what it means and to develop arguments for effective alternatives. Many scientists are worried that humanity is already bumping up against some natural limits. They say we will need to make big changes to how we live if we want to avoid causing more natural disasters in the future.

To create resilient and sustainable communities in the 21st century, we need literate citizens who question the economics fed by government and big business and then show viable, thriving alternatives in action. We need to get ambitious about scale and realistic about process.

A multi-currency world is already here and opens up new possibilities for us. Local currency activist Kevin Parcell sums this up in a Facebook conversation:

> The broad strategy of the community currency movement is the use of both local and global currencies, sometimes in the same transaction.
>
> The global marketplace is excellent at combining resources to give us global civilization, and when local marketplaces provide those resources sustainably then we will have a prosperous sustainable world.
>
> The seeming contradiction is resolved by creating local currencies that are stronger than global currencies so that communities are empowered to reclaim control of their destinies.

Other generations faced big challenges: the Industrial Revolution with its sweeping social and economic changes; abolishing slavery; defeating fascism; establishing civil rights for all. The generations now alive must solve the 'money problem'. We must reclaim money from the speculators and restore it to its role as a medium for trade that serves us all.

Resources to help you

Training, consulting and speaking on local currencies

I can guide you step-by-step through the process of designing and implementing a local currency in your community or region. This is the website for my services: www.valueforpeople.co.uk, and you can email me: info@valueforpeople.co.uk

Books

People Money – the Promise of Regional Currencies (2012)by Margrit Kennedy, Bernard Lietaer and John Rogers. This book gives an overview of the emerging global movement of local currencies. It includes profiles of 16 local currency leaders from around the world and is *a blueprint for how to start a currency*. One reviewer described it as the 'bible' of local currencies.

The End of Money and the Beginning of Civilisation (2010) by Thomas H Greco.

New Economics Foundation (nef)

The London based nef has been a key supporter of the Brixton and Bristol Pounds.It is currently host to the trans-European local currencies project Community Currencies in Action, led by Leander Bindewald: www.communitycurrenciesinaction.eu

The Reconomy Project from the Transition Network:

www.reconomy.org/

Questions for Study Groups

Chapter One

1. Do you think our region would benefit from a local currency?

2. What aspects of the local community, local resources and local wealth do we wish to support using a local currency?

3. Do you think Time Credits would be useful to our community? If so, what needs could be met?

Chapter Two

1. Did you know that privately owned banks have a monopoly on the creation of new money? Has this information affected the way you view the money supply?

2. What are the strengths of national currencies?

3. What are the main weaknesses of national currencies?

4. Why is debt a problem?

Chapter Three

1. What can a local currency do that other ideas for monetary reform can't?

2. Do you agree with any of the arguments *for* local currencies?

3. What does your inner sceptic say about local currencies?

4. What would convince you to use one?

Chapter Four

1. What is the importance of geographical and ethical boundaries for local currencies?

2. What have you learned from the different local currencies in action?

3. Which sustainable local currency design do you think would be most likely to succeed in our region?

Chapter Five

1. Do these answers convince you?

2. Would you be able to convince a sceptic?

Chapter Six

1. How would you support a local currency if there was one?

2. What do you think are the most important issues for currency organisers?

About the Author

 **John Rogers** cut his teeth with local currencies by running a local exchange system in Wales for 10 years. He co-founded the Wales Institute for Community Currencies at the University of Newport, which he directed with Geoff Thomas from 2003-2007. They coordinated research into the effects of time banking in ex-mining communities, which was published by the Joseph Rowntree Foundation in 'Hidden Work'.

John is co-author with Margrit Kennedy and Bernard Lietaer of *People Money - the Promise of Regional Currencies* and an Associate Scholar with the Institute for Leadership and Sustainability (IFLAS) at the University of Cumbria. He offers training and consulting for local currencies through Value for People and has spoken and led workshops at many international conferences. *www.valueforpeople.co.uk*

Many thanks to Leander Bindewald, Bruce Dickson, Kevin Parcell, Matthew Slater and Susan Steed, for their valuable suggestions for improvements, and to Triarchy Press and my patient editor Alison Melvin.

Lightning Source UK Ltd.
Milton Keynes UK
UKOW041547040613

211752UK00001B/1/P